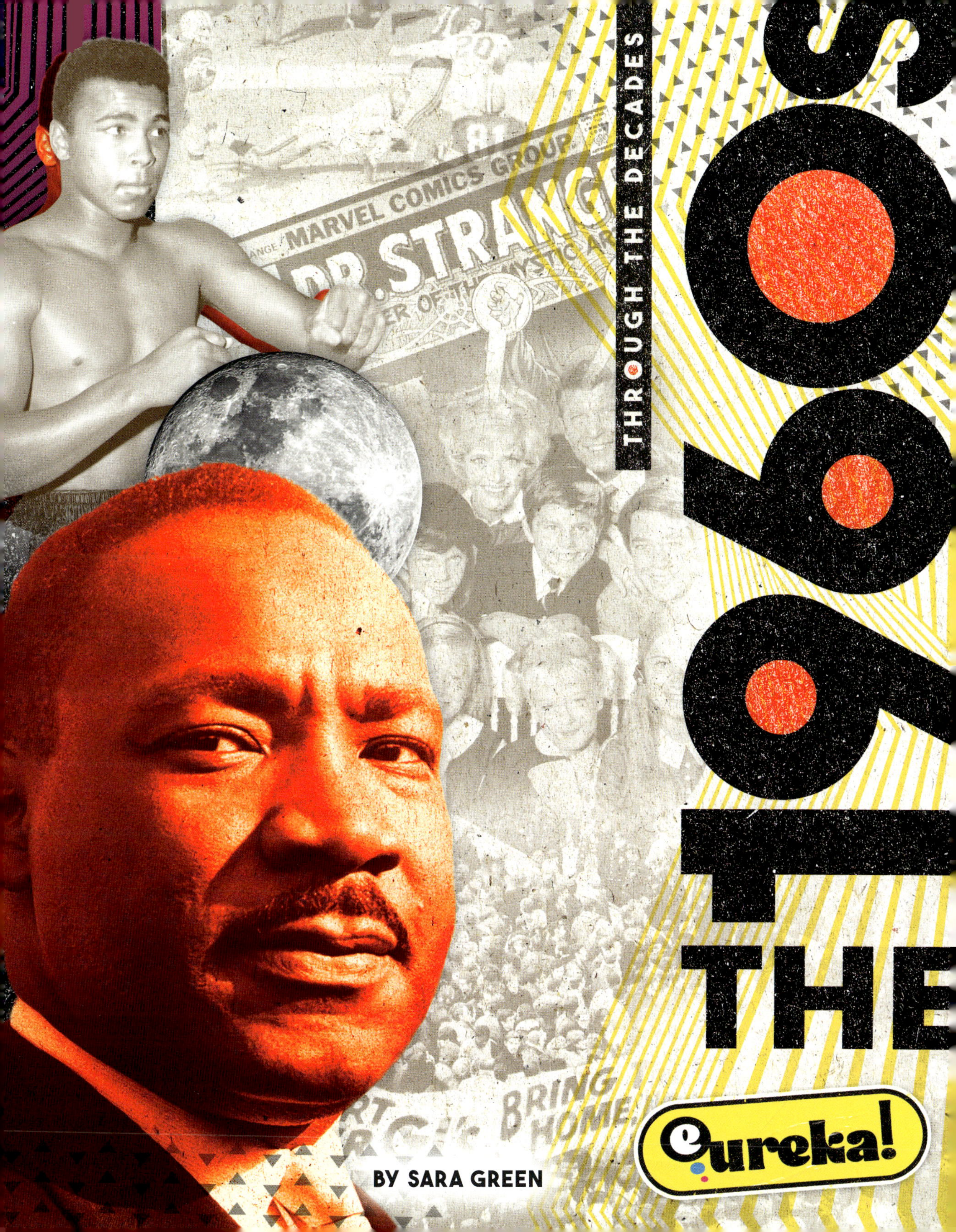
THROUGH THE DECADES
THE 1960s
MARVEL COMICS GROUP
DR. STRANGE
BY SARA GREEN
eureka!

Eureka!

Eureka! books turn real stories into unforgettable experiences. This nonfiction imprint sparks curiosity, encourages critical thinking, and engages middle-grade readers. *Eureka!* books empower young minds to explore the stories of the real world, one fascinating fact at a time. Unravel the power of knowledge and lifelong learning with *Eureka!*

This edition first published in 2026 by Bellwether Media, Inc.

Library of Congress Cataloging-in-Publication Data

LC record for The 1960s available at: https://lccn.loc.gov/2025021795

Editor: Rebecca Sabelko Designer: Andrea Schneider

Printed in the United States of America, North Mankato, MN.

TABLE OF CONTENTS

WELCOME TO THE 1960s!

It is Sunday, February 9, 1964. A girl has been waiting for this day for months! Tonight, the Beatles are appearing live on *The Ed Sullivan Show*. She has been a huge Beatles fan since she first heard them on the radio in December. "I Want to Hold Your Hand" is her favorite song.

The girl must wait a little longer to see the Fab Four. Her family has dinner at her grandmother's house each Sunday, and today is no different. The family piles into their station wagon and drives over to her grandmother's house. As the girl steps through the front door, she smells roast beef and apple pie. Her stomach rumbles. She even forgets about the Beatles for a moment!

That evening, the family gathers around the television. It is time to watch *The Ed Sullivan Show*. When Ed introduces the Beatles, the girl joins the television studio audience with screams of glee! The band launches into a song called "All My Loving." It quickly becomes the girl's new favorite song!

the Beatles performing on
The Ed Sullivan Show

WHAT HAPPENED IN THE 1960s?

The 1960s was a decade of turmoil, change, and growth. Around the world, violence raged as people tried to claim freedom from **colonial** powers. **Cold War** tensions between the United States and the **Soviet Union** brought the world to the brink of **nuclear war**. The Soviet threat of **communism** led the U.S. to become **entrenched** in the Vietnam War. The rivalry between the U.S. and Soviet Union had some positive outcomes. It ignited the Space Race and drove the first humans to walk on the Moon!

The civil rights, feminist, and anti-war movements grew stronger during the decade. People came together to challenge authority and fight for change. The decade also marked the beginning of the environmental movement, fueled by the public's awareness of threats to the earth. Many young people joined the hippie **counterculture**. They questioned traditional values about materialism and gender and chose a simpler, more peaceful lifestyle. Many of them experimented with new music, hairstyles, and fashions. The movements of the 1960s faced setbacks and tragedies, but they also improved many people's lives. They would impact people across the globe for generations to come.

illustration of Yuri Gagarin

FIRST IN SPACE

On April 12, 1961, Soviet cosmonaut Yuri Gagarin became the first human to travel successfully into space. His spacecraft, *Vostok 1*, made one orbit around Earth and returned to land after about 108 minutes.

HOW MUCH?

1 GALLON GAS
$0.31 (1960)
$0.34 (1969)

THE NEW YORK TIMES
(late city edition)
$0.05 (1960) | $0.10 (1969)

1 GALLON MILK
$0.36 (1960)
$0.47 (1969)

MOVIE TICKET
$0.75 (1960)
$1.42 (1969)

CANDY BAR
$0.05 (1960)
$0.10 (1969)

BOTTLE OF COKE
$0.10 (1960)
$0.10 (1969)

LOAF OF BREAD
$0.20 (1960)
$0.23 (1969)

HISTORY

UNITED STATES HISTORY

President John F. Kennedy's election in 1960 gave Americans hope for the future and inspired them to serve their country and the world. But President Kennedy faced major challenges. In 1961, the U.S. failed to overthrow the Cuban leader Fidel Castro in an invasion known as the Bay of Pigs. The next year, the Cuban Missile Crisis occurred. This confrontation between the U.S. and the Soviet Union over Soviet missiles in Cuba nearly led to nuclear war. Fortunately, the leaders of the two countries came to an agreement to end the crisis.

Major events encouraged by the Civil Rights Movement led to societal changes throughout the South. **LGBTQ+** activists took a stand against unjust treatment during the Stonewall Uprising. The six-day uprising protested police brutality and the unjust treatment of LGBTQ+ peoples.

PRESIDENT KENNEDY TAKING THE OATH OF OFFICE

CUBAN MISSILE CRISIS

STONEWALL UPRISING

Vietnam War protesters

President Kennedy shortly before his assassination

ASSASSINATIONS

In 1963, President Kennedy was assassinated in Dallas, Texas, while riding in an open car. Lee Harvey Oswald, the assassin, was shot and killed days later. In 1968, civil rights leader Martin Luther King Jr. was shot and killed in Memphis, Tennessee. That year, a gunman also murdered President Kennedy's brother Robert.

VIETNAM WAR DRAFT

In 1965, the U.S. entered the war in Vietnam, a small country in Southeast Asia. As the war escalated, President Johnson called for a draft. Many people did not support the draft, and thousands of men tried to avoid it. By the time the U.S. finally pulled out of Vietnam in 1973, the U.S. military had drafted around 2.2 million young men.

SUMMER OF LOVE

During the summer of 1967, around 100,000 people gathered in the Haight-Ashbury neighborhood in San Francisco, California, to spread the message of peace and love. This gathering is known as the Summer of Love.

UNITED STATES POLITICS

In 1960, John F. Kennedy narrowly defeated Richard Nixon to become the 35th president of the U.S. While in office, Kennedy established the Peace Corps and signed the Equal Pay Act of 1963. This law ended wage inequality based on gender. He also helped create the Limited Test Ban Treaty of 1963 to stop nuclear tests in the atmosphere, space, and underwater.

President John F. Kennedy

ELECTION SHOWDOWN: 1960 PRESIDENTIAL ELECTION

KENNEDY (DEMOCRATIC)
NIXON (REPUBLICAN)
BYRD

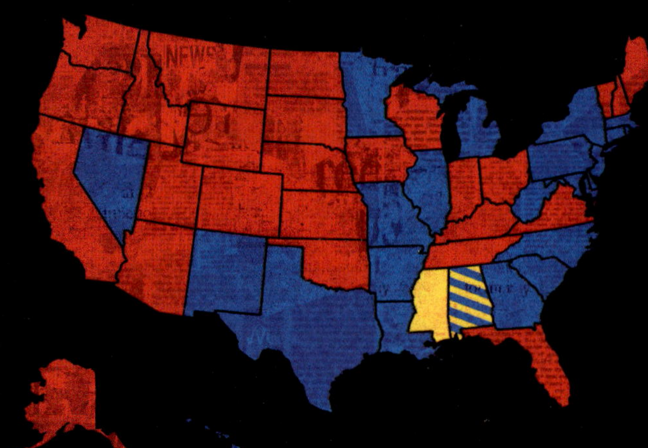

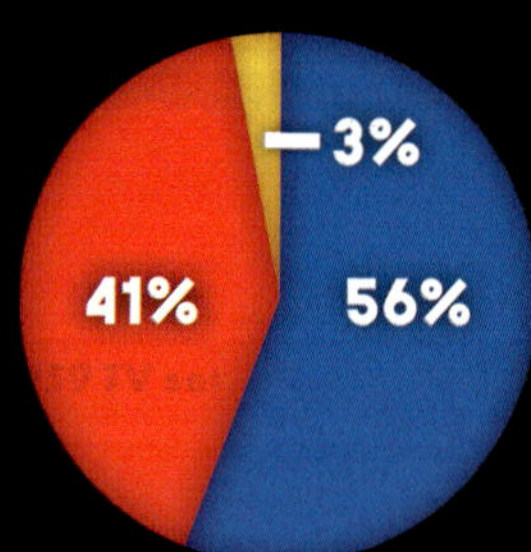

ELECTORAL VOTES

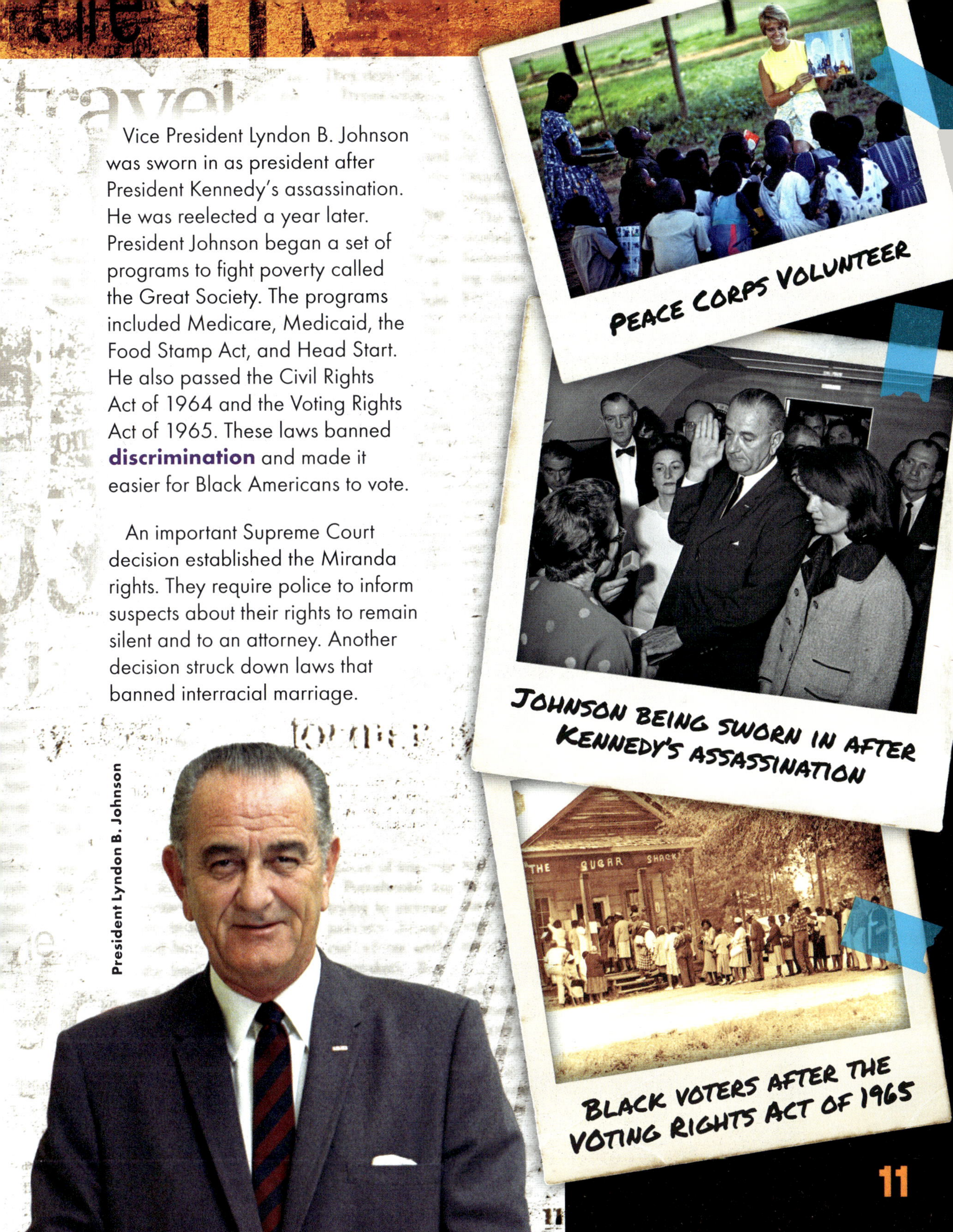

Vice President Lyndon B. Johnson was sworn in as president after President Kennedy's assassination. He was reelected a year later. President Johnson began a set of programs to fight poverty called the Great Society. The programs included Medicare, Medicaid, the Food Stamp Act, and Head Start. He also passed the Civil Rights Act of 1964 and the Voting Rights Act of 1965. These laws banned **discrimination** and made it easier for Black Americans to vote.

An important Supreme Court decision established the Miranda rights. They require police to inform suspects about their rights to remain silent and to an attorney. Another decision struck down laws that banned interracial marriage.

PEACE CORPS VOLUNTEER

JOHNSON BEING SWORN IN AFTER KENNEDY'S ASSASSINATION

BLACK VOTERS AFTER THE VOTING RIGHTS ACT OF 1965

President Lyndon B. Johnson

SPOTLIGHT ON:

THE MOON LANDING

On July 16, 1969, the Apollo 11 spacecraft launched from Cape Kennedy with astronauts Neil Armstrong, Edwin "Buzz" Aldrin, and Michael Collins on board. It took four days for Apollo 11 to reach the Moon. On July 20, 1969, Armstrong and Aldrin boarded *Eagle*, Apollo 11's **lunar module**, and descended to the Moon's surface. Collins remained in orbit in *Columbia*, the spacecraft's **command module**. A few hours later, Armstrong became the first person to set foot on the Moon, stating, "That's one small step for man, one giant leap for mankind." More than half a billion people around the world watched the event live on television.

Neil Armstrong and Edwin "Buzz" Aldrin on the Moon

MAKING HEADLINES

"Offices, banks, schools, to close for moon-walk"

—*The Miami News*, July 17, 1969

"MEN WALK ON MOON"

—*THE NEW YORK TIMES*, JULY 21, 1969

Aldrin soon joined Armstrong on the Moon's surface. The two men spent more than two hours taking photos and collecting samples. They also planted the U.S. flag in the lunar soil before returning to *Columbia*.

Apollo 11 spent more than two days in lunar orbit, circling the Moon 30 times. The crew returned safely to Earth on July 24, 1969. Today, scientists still study rock and soil samples from the Apollo 11 mission.

> "MEN WALK ON MOON! TRIUMPH FOR MANKIND"
>
> —*Milwaukee Sentinel*, July 21, 1969

WHO'S WHO?

NEIL ARMSTRONG

ROLE:
American astronaut

KNOWN FOR:
In 1969, Armstrong became the first person to walk on the Moon.

WORLD HISTORY

The 1960s saw sweeping change around the world. Political instability affected many countries in Latin America and Southeast Asia. Ongoing conflict between Israel and the Arab state led to the 1967 Six-Day War, or the Arab-Israeli War. Many African and Asian countries, including Algeria, Kenya, and Singapore, gained independence from colonial rule. A cultural revolution in China aimed to preserve communism. It led to widespread chaos and destruction in the country.

Meanwhile, the U.S. remained committed to stopping the spread of communism. This created more tension with the Soviet Union as well as other nations.

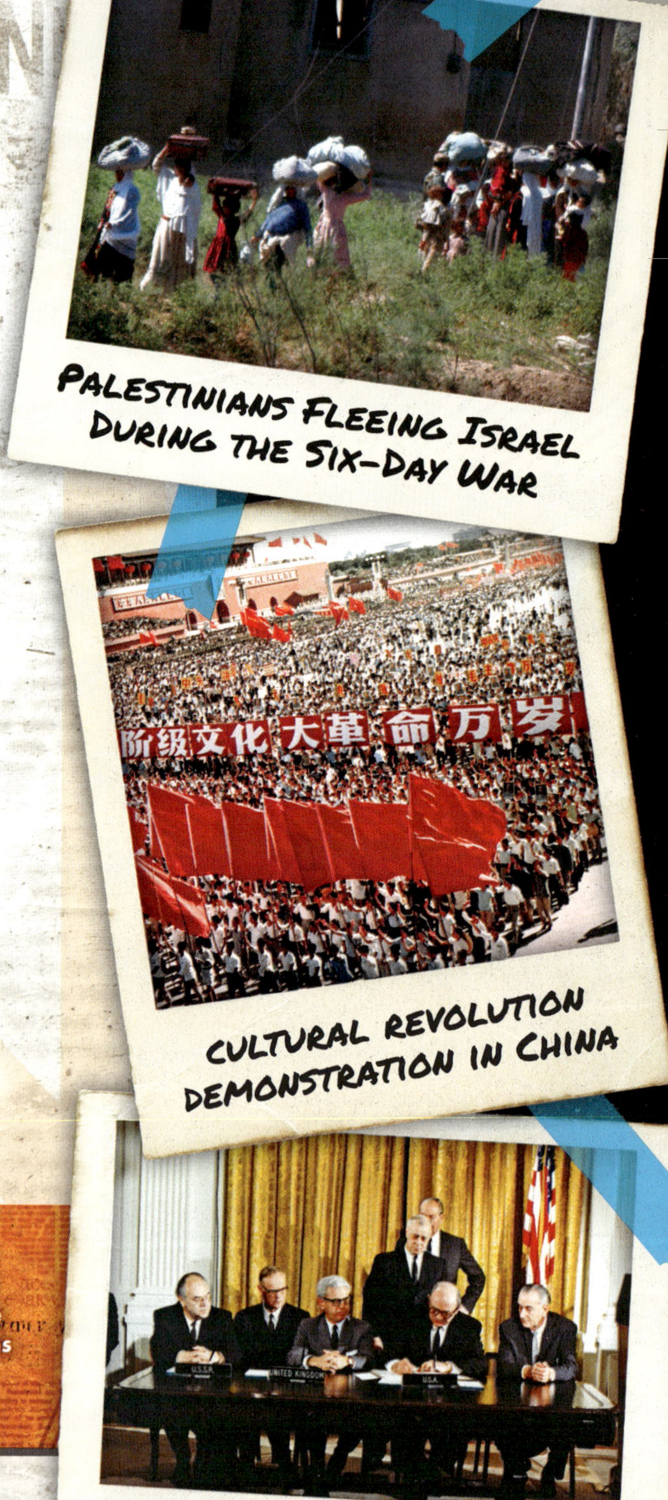

PALESTINIANS FLEEING ISRAEL DURING THE SIX-DAY WAR

CULTURAL REVOLUTION DEMONSTRATION IN CHINA

WORLD LEADERS SIGNING THE OUTER SPACE TREATY

OUTER SPACE TREATY

The U.S., Soviet Union, and around 60 other countries signed the Outer Space Treaty in 1967. It bans nuclear weapons from outer space. Today, over 100 countries have signed the treaty.

SIX-DAY WAR

Heightened tensions between Israel and neighboring Arab countries led to a brief war in 1967 called the Six-Day War. Israel gained a significant amount of territory, including the West Bank, the Gaza Strip, the Golan Heights, and the Sinai Peninsula.

BERLIN WALL

In 1961, the East German communist government began erecting a massive wall in Berlin to stop people from fleeing into capitalist West Germany. The Berlin Wall became one of the most prominent symbols of the Cold War. It remained in place until 1989 when it was torn down. Germany became one country again.

construction of the Berlin wall

CULTURAL REVOLUTION IN CHINA

In 1966, Mao Zedong, chairman of the Chinese Communist Party, launched the Cultural Revolution. Chairman Mao aimed to remove all remnants of capitalist and traditional elements from Chinese society. The movement led to widespread turmoil, persecution, and destruction across the country. It finally ended in 1976.

Mao Zedong

SPOTLIGHT ON:

VIETNAM WAR

Vietnam was split into the communist North and the non-communist South in 1954. The U.S. soon pledged support to South Vietnam. In 1961, the U.S. began sending troops to South Vietnam to help stop communists from gaining power. But a series of naval incidents in 1964 led to passing the Gulf of Tonkin Resolution. It allowed the U.S. to increase its military presence in Vietnam. The U.S. began bombing North Vietnam, and U.S. combat forces were sent to the country for battle.

More than 385,000 U.S. military personnel had been stationed in South Vietnam by the end of 1966. Deaths of Vietnamese and U.S. troops rose steadily. Some people from the U.S. began questioning the reasons for the war. Horrific images of battles fueled the anti-war movement in the U.S.

Peace talks began in 1968, but five more years of **carnage** would follow. The U.S. pulled out of Vietnam in 1973. On April 30, 1975, North Vietnamese tanks rolled into Saigon, the South Vietnamese capital, and took control. The country was unified under communist rule as the Socialist Republic of Vietnam.

MAKING HEADLINES

"SPRAY KILLING OF ENEMY'S CROPS STEPPED UP BY U.S. IN VIETNAM"

—*THE NEW YORK TIMES*, JULY 26, 1966

"Massive U.S. Anti-War Protest; Rallies, Marches in Bay Area"

—*San Francisco Chronicle*, Thursday, October 16, 1969

"FIERCE BATTLES ERUPT IN VIETNAM; CLASHES DISRUPT VIETCONG'S NEW YEAR'S CEASE-FIRE"

—*THE NEW YORK TIMES*, DECEMBER 31, 1969

NORTH VIETNAM AFTER BEING BOMBED

U.S. MILITARY SPRAYING HARMFUL CHEMICALS OVER VIETNAMESE JUNGLES

U.S. SOLDIERS ARRIVING IN VIETNAM

SOCIAL CHANGES

The 1960s was a time of major social change. Hundreds of thousands of people used their voices and actions to reshape society. Black Americans fought for racial equality through protests, marches, and **sit-ins**. Activists called Freedom Riders rode buses throughout the South to protest legalized **racism** in 1961. The 1963 March on Washington drew around 250,000 people in support of civil rights. Martin Luther King Jr. delivered his celebrated "I Have a Dream" speech. It called for an end to racism. Two years later, King led thousands of people on a series of marches in Alabama to protest the state's lack of civil rights. The marches led to the passage of the Voting Rights Act of 1965.

Martin Luther King Jr. at the March on Washington

Other groups also gained strength during the decade. The National Organization for Women was founded in 1966 to promote equal rights and equal pay for women. A series of demonstrations at The Stonewall Inn in New York City marked the reignited gay rights movement. The number of anti-war marches and rallies spread across the country as the decade progressed. Colleges and universities became centers of political activism, and many student groups played leading roles in organizing protests.

THE WASHINGTON FREEDOM RIDERS COMMITTEE

1963 MARCH ON WASHINGTON

NATIONAL ORGANIZATION FOR WOMEN PROTEST

James Meredith

COURAGE TO ENROLL

In September 1962, James Meredith enrolled as the first Black student at the University of Mississippi. Riots erupted on campus that left two people dead and hundreds wounded. President Kennedy sent in federal troops to stop the violence and protect Meredith.

SCIENCE AND TECHNOLOGY

TECHNOLOGY

The 1969 moon landing is one of the greatest technological achievements of all time. Other groundbreaking advances of the 1960s included **integrated circuits**. These allowed computers to be smaller, faster, and have more functions. The first light-emitting diode (LED) to produce visible light was invented in 1962. LEDs were first used as special lights in small electronics. They have since grown to be the most widely used type of light! A powerful material called Kevlar was invented in 1965. It replaced steel wires in car tires. It would later be used to make canoes, bulletproof vests, helmets, and many other products! Cordless tools, cassette tapes, and the automated teller machine, or ATM, also got their starts in the 1960s!

calculator with LEDs in the screen

911

WHAT IS IT?:
A universal telephone number for U.S. citizens to request emergency assistance

INVENTOR:
The Federal Communications Commission and the American Telephone and Telegraph Company

YEAR INVENTED:
1968

EFFECT ON DAILY LIFE:
Increased public safety by making emergency services readily available to anyone with a telephone and accelerated the speed of emergency responses in critical situations

The decade saw the beginning of the modern Internet. In 1969, the U.S. Department of Defense created a computer network called Advanced Research Projects Agency Network, or ARPANET. It was the first digital network to share information between computers over long distances using telephone lines. ARPANET was mainly used for research, military, and academic purposes.

wheat field in India with a watering system from the Green Revolution

THE GREEN REVOLUTION

The Green Revolution was a program introduced in the 1960s to combat world hunger. Farmers began to use new chemicals and seeds to increase their yields of wheat, maize, and rice. This led to larger food supplies, particularly in Latin America and Asia.

MEDICAL SCIENCE

The 1960s saw great advances in medicine. Many dramatic breakthroughs focused on the heart. The decade saw the first heart valve replacement surgery and the first successful coronary artery bypass surgery. In 1967, South African surgeon Dr. Christiaan Barnard performed the first successful human heart transplant on Louis Washkansky, a man dying of heart disease. Washkansky only lived 18 days, but the surgery paved the way for future developments in transplant surgery. These techniques would go on to save thousands of lives over time.

Dr. Christiaan Barnard

THE PILL

The FDA approved the birth control pill in 1960. It gave women control over their reproduction and more freedom to pursue education and careers.

An oral polio vaccine developed by Dr. Albert Sabin became available in the U.S. in 1961. It made mass **immunization** easy. The first measles vaccine became available in 1963 and significantly reduced the number of cases of this deadly disease. By the late 1960s, vaccines were also available to protect against mumps and rubella. Over time, these vaccines have saved millions of lives worldwide.

The dangers of cigarette smoking gained more recognition in the 1960s. In 1964, the Surgeon General's report on smoking and health called for public campaigns to reduce smoking. Soon, cigarette packages began to include health warnings about the risks of smoking. Their purpose was to motivate people to quit smoking and discourage people from starting to smoke.

WASHKANSKY RECOVERING AFTER A HEART TRANSPLANT

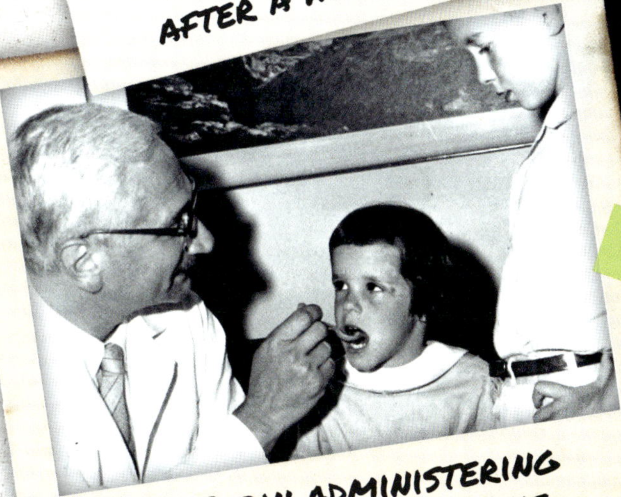

DR. SABIN ADMINISTERING AN ORAL POLIO VACCINE

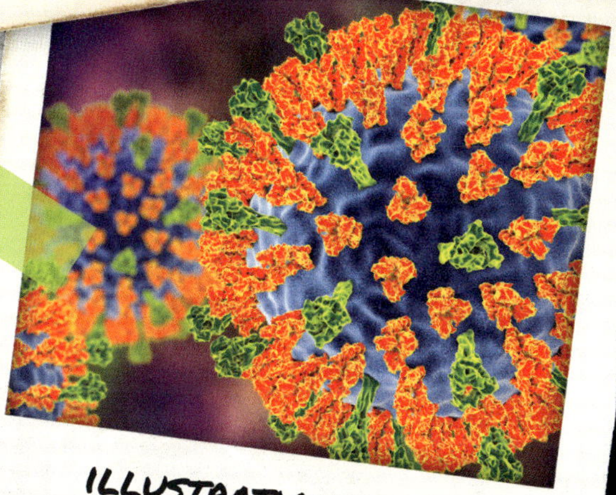

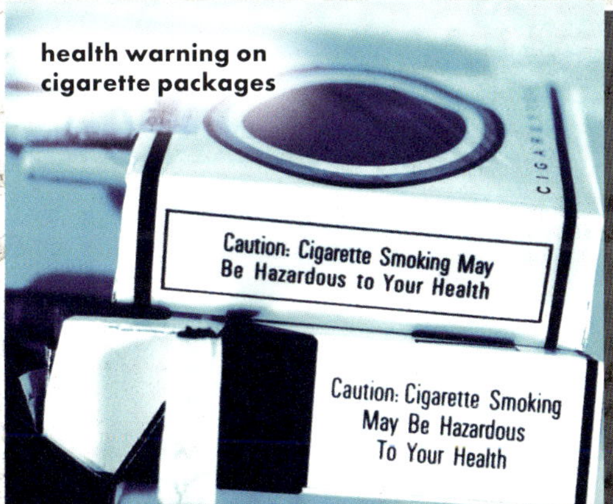

health warning on cigarette packages

ILLUSTRATION OF THE MEASLES VIRUS

DAILY LIFE

LIFE IN THE '60s

A new focus on women's rights in the 1960s affected many people's lives. Early in the decade, many families followed a traditional model. Men were the head of the household. They were expected to have careers and provide for their family. Women raised their children and managed the home. However, advances in women's rights led people to defy traditions. Many women began attending college and entering the workforce.

Suburban areas continued to grow dramatically during the decade, fueled by the affordability of homes and cars. Fast-food chains like McDonald's expanded. They offered quick and affordable meals for families. Kids enjoyed riding their banana bikes, listening to the Beatles, and watching *American Bandstand* on TV. **Overhead projectors** and educational movies and filmstrips were often part of their school days.

The growing interstate highway system led to the rise of the family road trip. Families drove across the country to explore new places. Many camped outside or stayed at roadside motels along highways!

McDONALD'S

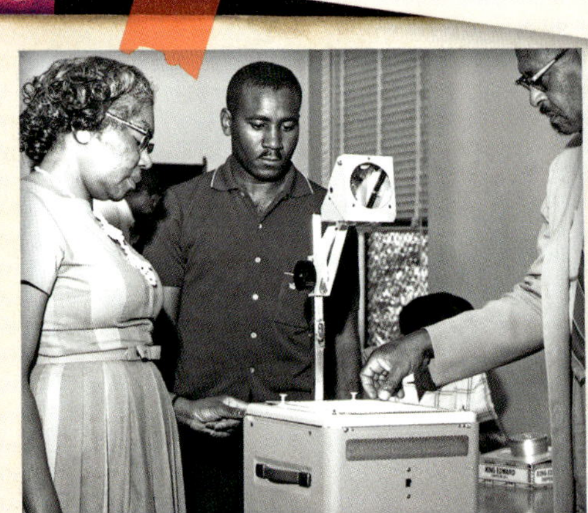
OVERHEAD PROJECTOR

WOMEN GRADUATING FROM COLLEGE

1960s SLANG

to understand or agree with something

Split

to leave quickly

Lay it on me

What is on your mind?

RIGHT ON!

used to enthusiastically agree with something

THREADS

clothes

FASHION TRENDS

Twiggy

Fashions ranged from chic and elegant to vibrant and funky in the '60s. Early in the decade, many women copied the elegance of First Lady Jacqueline Kennedy. She helped popularize tailored dresses, pencil skirts, and pillbox hats. As the decade progressed, fashion became more casual and innovative. Miniskirts, introduced in the mid-1960s by designer Mary Quant, became a symbol of youthful freedom. The look was often completed with white go-go boots. The sleeveless shift dress was another closet staple, while bell-bottom jeans and **psychedelic** prints were popular hippie fashions!

THE FACE OF THE 60s

Lesley Lawson, known as Twiggy, was one of the most famous models of the 1960s. Her thin frame, pixie haircut, and heavy eye makeup represented the decade's "Mod" look.

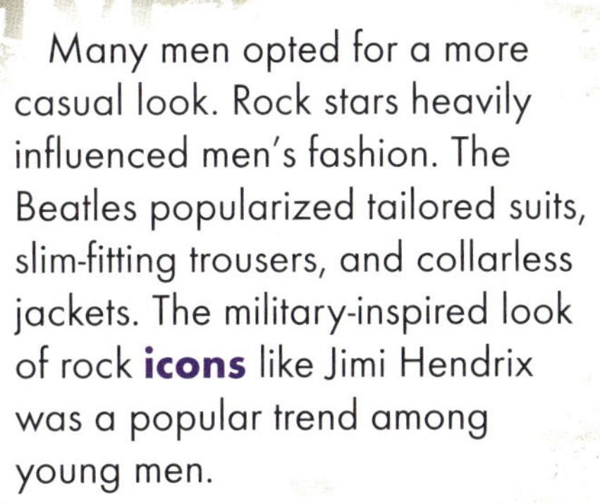

Many men opted for a more casual look. Rock stars heavily influenced men's fashion. The Beatles popularized tailored suits, slim-fitting trousers, and collarless jackets. The military-inspired look of rock **icons** like Jimi Hendrix was a popular trend among young men.

Hairstyles reflected the changing times. Short bobs and pixie cuts were in style. Women who embraced the counterculture often wore long hair. Popular men's hairstyles ranged from the Beatles' mop tops to shaggy hippie looks. The Afro hairstyle became an expression of pride and a symbol of freedom within the Black community.

JACQUELINE KENNEDY WEARING A PILLBOX HAT

JIMI HENDRIX WEARING A MILITARY-INSPIRED JACKET

Afro hairstyle

THE BEATLES WITH MOP TOP HAIRSTYLES

PRODUCTS AND TOYS

The growing economy coupled with high birth rates and increased TV marketing led to a surge in toy sales in the 1960s. The increased use of inexpensive plastic also had a huge impact on toy production. Toy makers began making toys in greater quantities than ever before!

G.I. JOE

G.I. Joe was launched by Hasbro in 1964. Hasbro invented the term "action figure" to market the toy to boys. G.I. Joe came in uniforms representing the four branches of the U.S. Armed Forces. Hasbro released an astronaut G.I. Joe in 1966.

ETCH A SKETCH

This mechanical drawing toy was introduced in 1960. Children created images by turning two knobs that moved an internal stylus. They erased their creations by shaking the toy. Etch A Sketch was one of the best-selling toys of the 1960s.

SPIROGRAPH

Spirograph is a geometric drawing toy introduced by Kenner in 1966. Each Spirograph kit included a variety of plastic wheels, rings, and bars, as well as two ballpoint pens. Kids used these items to draw countless patterns on paper!

CHATTY CATHY

Chatty Cathy was a talking doll introduced by Mattel in 1960. Children pulled a string on her back to hear the doll say phrases such as "let's play school" and "I love you." The original doll had blonde hair and blue eyes. A Black doll and a doll with brunette hair were introduced a few years later.

EASY-BAKE OVEN

The Easy-Bake Oven was introduced in 1963. It allowed children to bake real cakes and brownies using a small light bulb as a heat source. The oven also came with cake and cookie mixes, a recipe book, baking pans, and utensils.

HOT WHEELS

Hot Wheels is a line of toy cars and trucks launched by Mattel in 1968. The models looked authentic and zoomed fast. Mattel also created flexible, plastic tracks with a signature loop for racing Hot Wheels. Kids loved the miniature cars. Sales topped $16 million in the first year!

TROLL DOLLS

Troll dolls were invented by a Danish woodworker in the 1950s. By 1962, they had become an international sensation! Kids adored their wild, colorful hair and funny faces. More than one million troll dolls were sold in the U.S. by 1964!

ARTS AND ENTERTAINMENT

PUBLICATIONS

The **turbulence** of the 1960s inspired some of the decade's best authors. Many of their books tackled women's rights, civil rights, and the counterculture movement. Author Rachel Carson is credited with sparking the environmental movement with her book *Silent Spring*. It highlights the dangers of pesticide use.

Many classic children's books were also published during the decade. Mauric Sendak introduced readers to Max and the Wild Things in *Where the Wild Things Are*. Theodor Geisel, known as Dr. Seuss, used a list of only 50 words to write *Green Eggs and Ham*!

Magazines celebrated the decade. *TIME* magazine's "Person of the Year" honorees included John F. Kennedy, Martin Luther King Jr., and U.S. scientists. The first issue of *Rolling Stone* hit the newsstands in 1967 with musician John Lennon on the cover. The magazine's focus on music, popular culture, and politics made it a favorite for teens and young adults.

READING REC

TITLE:
A WRINKLE IN TIME

AUTHOR:
Madeleine L'Engle

YEAR PUBLISHED:
1962

SUMMARY:
Meg Murry, Charles Wallace Murry, and Calvin O'Keefe must travel through space and time to rescue the Murrys' father from the evil forces that hold him prisoner on a faraway planet.

CHARLIE AND THE CHOCOLATE FACTORY

This beloved classic by British author Roald Dahl tells the story of Willy Wonka, a quirky candymaker, and the five children who win the chance to tour his chocolate factory. The book has sold at least 20 million copies worldwide. It was later adapted into movies, an opera, and a musical.

THE OUTSIDERS

S.E. Hinton was only 16 years old when she wrote *The Outsiders*. This gritty coming-of-age novel about the conflicts between social classes and family relationships would become one of the most influential young adult books of all time. It has been translated into more than 30 languages. The book was adapted into a film in 1983, a television series in 1990, and a musical in 2024.

TO KILL A MOCKINGBIRD

Harper Lee's *To Kill a Mockingbird* addresses the themes of racial injustice and morality through the eyes of a young white girl in the American South. It won a Pulitzer Prize in 1961 and was adapted into an Academy Award-winning film in 1962. Today, the novel is considered an American literary classic.

Spider-Man

MARVEL COMICS

Marvel Comics introduced many popular superheroes during the 1960s. Fans met Spider-Man, Iron Man, the Incredible Hulk, Thor, and Dr. Strange for the first time! The X-Men and the Fantastic Four also debuted in the '60s, along with Daredevil, Black Panther, and Silver Surfer.

MOVIES

The 1960s began with a slump in movie attendance. Television was now people's favorite form of entertainment. Moviemakers were forced to find new ways to draw audiences back to theaters. Some found success with big-budget epic films such as *Lawrence of Arabia* and *Doctor Zhivago*. Films that pushed creative boundaries also did well at the box office. *Guess Who's Coming to Dinner* openly tackled issues of race, while anti-war views were reflected in films such as *Dr. Strangelove*.

The Motion Picture Association of America (MPAA) rolled out its ratings system in 1968. Its goal was to help parents decide which movies were appropriate for their children to watch based on their content. The first MPAA ratings in 1968 were G for general audiences, M for mature, R for restricted, and X for adult. The M rating later became PG for parental guidance.

MUSICALS

Musicals were popular in the 1960s. Films such as *West Side Story, The Sound of Music,* and *My Fair Lady* were massive hits and won numerous Academy Awards. The decade also saw the rise of youth-oriented musicals such as *A Hard Day's Night,* featuring the Beatles and rock and roll music.

AT THE BOX OFFICE

TOP-GROSSING FILMS OF THE 1960s

- ***The Sound of Music* (1965)**
- ***The Graduate* (1967)**
- ***Butch Cassidy and the Sundance Kid* (1969)**
- ***The Jungle Book* (1967)**
- ***My Fair Lady* (1964)**
- ***Thunderball* (1965)**
- ***Cleopatra* (1963)**
- ***2001: A Space Odyssey* (1968)**
- ***Guess Who's Coming to Dinner* (1967)**
- ***How the West Was Won* (1962)**

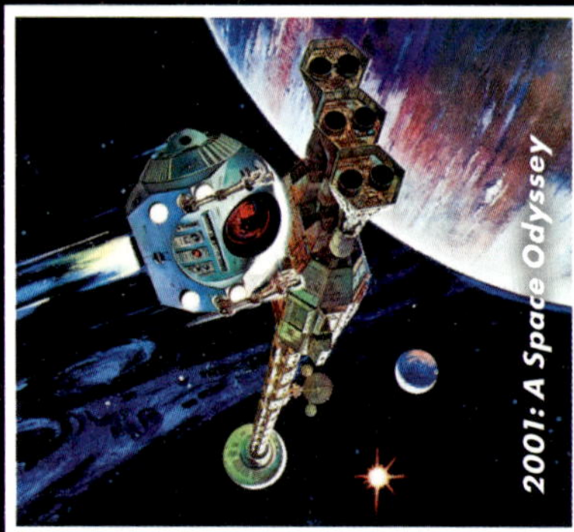
2001: A Space Odyssey

Sean Connery in *Dr. No*

MARY POPPINS

Mary Poppins, starring Julie Andrews and Dick Van Dyke, was a musical fantasy released by Walt Disney Studios in 1964. It was a smash hit and earned five Academy Awards, including Best Song for "Chim Chim Cher-ee." Its use of live action combined with animation charmed audiences around the world.

Julie Andrews as Mary Poppins

JAMES BOND FRANCHISE

The spy James Bond, played by actor Sean Connery, was introduced to movie audiences in the 1960s starting with *Dr. No* in 1962. *Goldfinger* and *Thunderball* were popular sequels.

SPECIAL EFFECTS

New standards were set for visual storytelling during the 1960s. Films such as *2001: A Space Odyssey* and *Planet of the Apes* revolutionized filmmaking with groundbreaking special effects. The use of miniatures, stop-motion animation, makeup, and other techniques paved the way for more advanced special effects in later decades.

ONE HUNDRED AND ONE DALMATIANS

Disney Studios released the animated film *One Hundred and One Dalmatians* in 1961. It was the year's highest-grossing film! The animators used a groundbreaking style of animation called the Xerox process to make the film. It would become the standard in animation for decades to follow. The character Cruella de Vil became a classic villain!

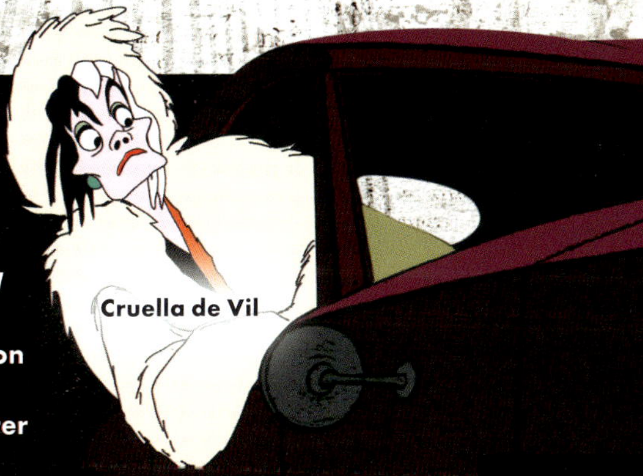
Cruella de Vil

TELEVISION

Television was the top source of entertainment during the 1960s. By 1960, most American homes had one television set with three channels to choose from. It was common for families to gather around the TV after dinner to watch their favorite programs.

Television not only entertained people. It also brought political and cultural events directly into their homes, especially after news broadcasts expanded from 15 minutes to 30 minutes in 1963. People could watch major events unfold. The Vietnam War was the first war to be widely televised. Coverage of its harsh realities significantly influenced public opinion of the war.

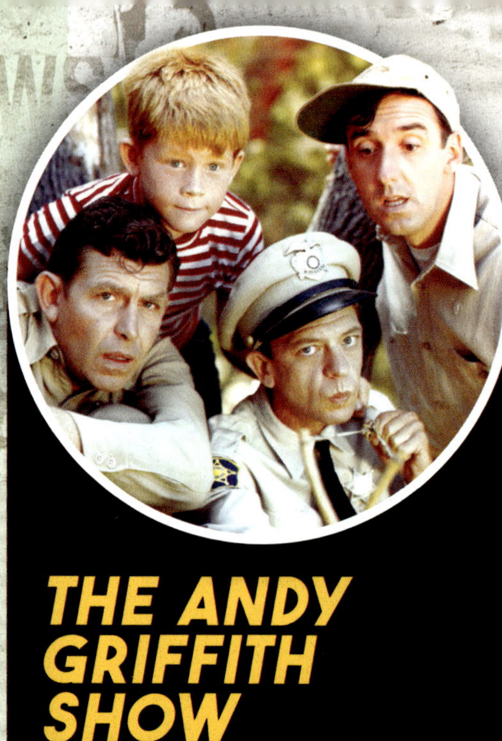

THE ANDY GRIFFITH SHOW

The sitcom *The Andy Griffith Show* was among the decade's most popular television series. It ran from 1960 to 1968. Set in the fictional town of Mayberry, the series followed the lives of Sheriff Andy Taylor, his son Opie, and the citizens of Mayberry. The show is known for its heartwarming stories and wholesome characters.

THE FIRST KENNEDY-NIXON DEBATE

On September 26, 1960, around 70 million people watched the presidential debate between John F. Kennedy and Richard Nixon. It was the first televised presidential debate in the U.S. Kennedy looked confident while Nixon appeared sickly. The power of television images became clear that evening. Viewers thought Kennedy had won, while radio listeners said Nixon had won.

Richard Nixon

STAR TREK

Star Trek, a sci-fi series created by Gene Roddenberry, debuted in 1966. It featured a multiracial cast and covered race, religion, war, and other social issues as the crew explored space in the starship USS *Enterprise*. The original series kicked off a franchise that included many spin-off series, feature films, books, games, and toys.

EDUCATIONAL PROGRAMMING

The 1960s saw the debut of two popular children's programs. *Mister Rogers' Neighborhood* debuted in 1968 followed by *Sesame Street* a year later. These programs entertained and educated countless children, while helping them feel good about themselves and their communities. They continue to inspire children's programming today.

Sesame Street

The Flintstones

ANIMATED FAVORITES

Many beloved cartoons were launched in the 1960s. *The Flintstones* ran from 1960 to 1966 and was the first successful primetime animated series. *The Jetsons*, *The Bugs Bunny/Road Runner Hour*, and *Scooby-Doo, Where Are You!* are other popular cartoons that debuted during the decade.

MUSIC

The 1960s was an exciting decade for music. The **British Invasion**, led by the Beatles and the Rolling Stones, revolutionized the music scene. Folk, psychedelic, and several other **genres** were forces for change within socio-political movements. Singer-songwriters such as Bob Dylan would leave a lasting mark on the history of music.

Surf rock, popularized by bands such as the Beach Boys and Jan and Dean, was inspired by Southern California's surfing scene. Its bright electric guitar sounds were meant to make listeners think of crashing ocean waves.

WOODSTOCK

The Woodstock Music and Art Fair began on August 15, 1969, on a farm in New York. More than 400,000 people attended this festival billed as "3 days of Peace & Music." Memorable performers included Richie Havens and Joe Cocker. Jimi Hendrix made history with his rendition of "The Star-Spangled Banner."

1960s PLAYLIST

- ***I'm Sorry***
  Brenda Lee (1960)
- ***Hello, Dolly!***
  Louis Armstrong (1964)
- ***My Girl***
  The Temptations (1964)
- ***Good Vibrations***
  The Beach Boys (1966)
- ***I'm A Believer***
  The Monkees (1966)
- ***Respect***
  Aretha Franklin (1967)
- ***All Along the Watchtower***
  Jimi Hendrix (1968)
- ***Hey Jude***
  The Beatles (1968)
- ***(Sittin' On) The Dock of the Bay***
  Otis Redding (1968)
- ***Sugar, Sugar***
  The Archies (1969)

Woodstock Music and Art Fair

FOLK MUSIC

The 1960s folk music scene blended traditional folk music with political and social commentary. The genre became closely associated with the civil rights movement and anti-war protests. Bob Dylan, Joan Baez, and Phil Ochs are some of the decade's most popular folk artists.

Bob Dylan

THE BEATLES

The Beatles were an English rock band with an innovative sound and style. The band included Paul McCartney, John Lennon, George Harrison, and Ringo Starr. A fan-led culture called Beatlemania swept the U.S. after the band appeared on *The Ed Sullivan Show* in 1964. Today, many Beatles hits, including "Let It Be" and "Yesterday," remain classics.

PSYCHEDELIC ROCK

Psychedelic rock is characterized by its experimental use of electronic effects. It is often associated with the counterculture movement. Bands such as the Doors and Jefferson Airplane gained millions of fans with their unusual lyrics and innovative sounds.

THE SUPREMES

The Supremes were a pop-soul vocal group who ranked among the most successful performers of the 1960s. The founding members of the Supremes were Diana Ross, Florence Ballard, Cindy Birdsong, and Mary Wilson. They got their first number one hit in 1964 with "Where Did Our Love Go." The group continued to top the charts through the decade.

U.S. SPORTS

The sports world was packed with action during the 1960s. Fans witnessed intense rivalries, dramatic moments, and remarkable achievements. Sports heroes such as boxer Muhammad Ali, football quarterback Joe Namath, and baseball pitcher Sandy Koufax became household names.

Professional football was beginning to overcome baseball as the most popular sport in the U.S. On January 15, 1967, millions of people watched the Green Bay Packers defeat the Kansas City Chiefs in the first Super Bowl.

The Special Olympics began in 1968, allowing children and adults with intellectual disabilities to participate in sports. It empowered millions of athletes to learn new skills and gain confidence.

MVP

NAME:
BILL RUSSELL

SPORT:
Basketball

TEAM:
Boston Celtics

YEARS ACTIVE:
1956 to 1969

KNOWN FOR:
An outstanding defender and leader, Bill Russell was one of the greatest basketball players of all time, winning 11 championships from 1957 to 1969, with the last 2 titles as player-coach.

NBA PIONEER

In 1966, Bill Russell became the first Black head coach in the NBA while still playing for the Celtics. He also coached the Seattle SuperSonics from 1973 to 1977 and the Sacramento Kings from 1987 to 1988.

Sandy Koufax accepting the Cy Yound Award

MAJOR MLB MOMENTS

Roger Maris and Mickey Mantle raced to beat Babe Ruth's season 60-hit home run record in 1961. Maris topped the record with 61 home runs! Sandy Koufax was a star pitcher for the Los Angeles Dodgers. In the 1960s, he won three Cy Young Awards for best pitcher in Major League Baseball (MLB) and pitched four no-hitters, including a perfect game.

Muhammad Ali

MUHAMMAD ALI

At 22, Cassius Clay defeated Sonny Liston in 1964 to win the World Heavyweight Championship. A few weeks later, Clay changed his name to Muhammad Ali. Known for his skills and charisma, Muhammad Ali successfully defended his title multiple times.

NBA GREATS

The Boston Celtics dominated the National Basketball Association (NBA) in the 1960s. The team, led by Bill Russell, won nine championships to become one of the greatest dynasties in sports history. Wilt Chamberlain was a commanding basketball player during the 1960s. He set numerous records, including scoring 100 points in a single game in 1962.

Vince Lombardi

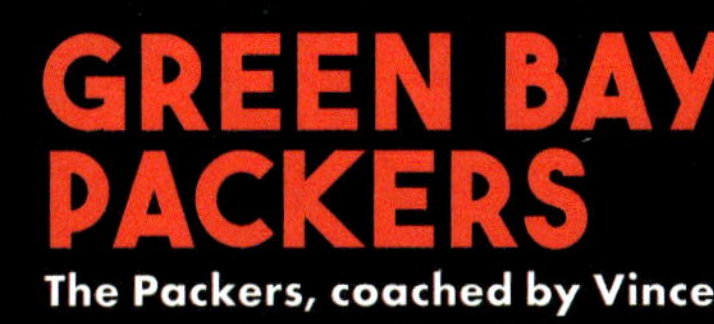

GREEN BAY PACKERS

The Packers, coached by Vince Lombardi, won five National Football League (NFL) Championships during the 1960s, including the first two Super Bowls. The team's success made the Packers a legendary name in professional football.

GLOBAL SPORTS

The 1960s are known for spectacular international sporting events and champion athletes. Many of them emerged from the six Olympics Games held during the decade. The 1960 Summer Olympics held in Rome, Italy, were notable for the debut of several sports legends. Cassius Clay, who later changed his name to Muhammad Ali, won gold in boxing. Wilma Rudolph made history by becoming the first American woman to win three gold medals in track and field in a single Olympics. Ethiopian Abebe Bikila won the marathon while running barefoot.

American sprinters Tommie Smith and John Carlos stunned fans worldwide in the 1968 Summer Olympics. They raised their fists during the medal ceremony for the 200-meter race to protest racial injustice in the U.S. This was just one of many monumental events that reflected the social, political, and cultural changes happening around the world.

OLYMPICS OF THE 1960s

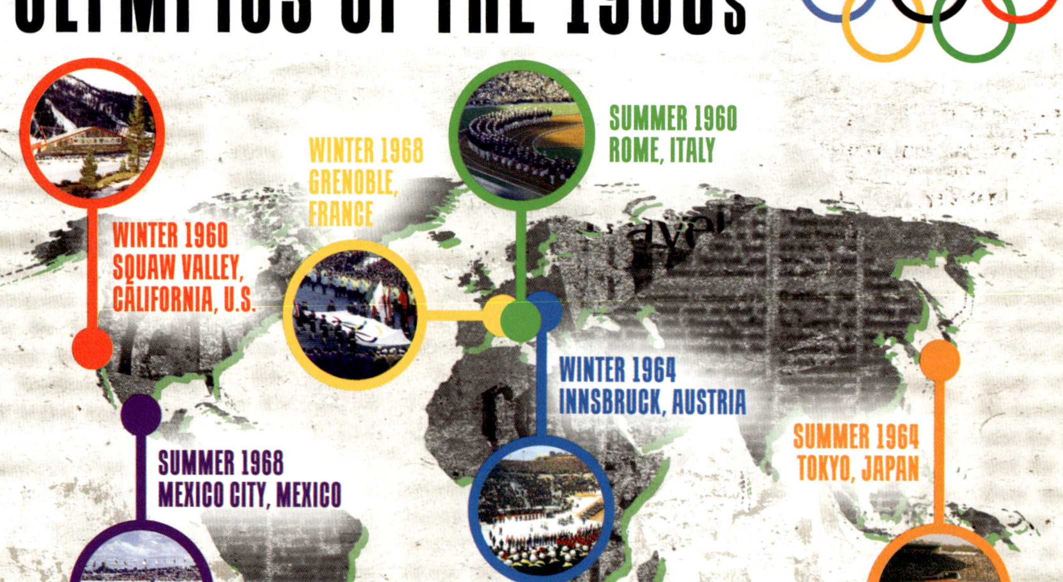

judo

1964 SUMMER OLYMPICS

The 1964 Summer Olympics were held in Tokyo, Japan. They were the first Olympics held in Asia. Judo and volleyball were introduced as Olympic sports during these games. They were also the first Olympics to broadcast live via satellite and became known as the "TV Olympics."

ROD LAVER

Australian tennis player Rod Laver is considered one of the greatest tennis players in history. In 1962 and 1969, he won the Grand Slam, or all four major tennis tournaments, in a single year. He is the only player in tennis history to win two calendar Grand Slams in singles!

Rod Laver

MONTREAL CANADIENS

The Montreal Canadiens dominated the National Hockey League (NHL) during the 1960s. The team won five Stanley Cups during the decade, making them one of the most successful teams in NHL history.

FRANCIS CHICHESTER

Francis Chichester was a British aviator and sailor. He won the first solo transatlantic yacht race in 1960. In 1966, he embarked on a solo sailing voyage around the world. He completed the voyage in 1967 to become the first person to sail around the world alone.

TIMELINE

FEBRUARY 1, 1960

Four Black college students carry out a sit-in at the Woolworth's lunch counter in Greensboro, North Carolina, sparking sit-ins across the nation to protest segregation

SEPTEMBER 26, 1960

John F. Kennedy and Richard Nixon participate in the first live televised presidential debate in the U.S.

AUGUST 13, 1961

Construction of the Berlin Wall begins

FEBRUARY 20, 1962

John Glenn becomes the first American to orbit Earth

APRIL 12, 1961

Yuri Gagarin, a Soviet cosmonaut, becomes the first human to orbit Earth

MAY 6, 1960

President Dwight D. Eisenhower signs the Civil Rights Act of 1960 into law

DECEMBER 11, 1961

The U.S. sends helicopters to support South Vietnam, marking what many believe to be America's entry into the Vietnam War

SEPTEMBER 30, 1962

A race riot erupts at the University of Mississippi to protest the enrollment of James Meredith, a Black man, at the all-white school

AUGUST 28, 1963
Martin Luther King Jr. delivers his "I Have a Dream" speech at the March on Washington in Washington, D.C.

AUGUST 27, 1964
Walt Disney's *Mary Poppins* has its world premiere in Los Angeles, California

OCTOBER 16, 1962
The 13-day Cuban Missile Crisis begins after the U.S. identifies Soviet missiles in Cuba

JANUARY 11, 1964
The U.S. Surgeon General announces that cigarette smoking causes cancer and heart disease

NOVEMBER 22, 1963
President John F. Kennedy is assassinated in Dallas, Texas

JUNE 10, 1963
President John F. Kennedy signs the Equal Pay Act

FEBRUARY 9, 1964
The Beatles make their first appearance on American television on *The Ed Sullivan Show*

1965
Kevlar is developed by American chemist Stephanie Kwolek at DuPont

MARCH 7, 1965
A series of three marches from Selma, Alabama, to Montgomery, Alabama, begins to protest the denial of Black Americans' right to vote

FEBRUARY 21, 1965
Malcom X, a key figure in the Civil Rights Movement, is assassinated

JULY 30, 1965
President Lyndon B. Johnson signs the Medicare and Medicaid Act, providing health insurance for the elderly and people with limited incomes

APRIL 18, 1966
The Sound of Music wins the Academy Award for Best Picture

MAY 1966
Mao Zedong launches the Cultural Revolution in China

JUNE 5 TO 10, 1967
The Six-Day War between Israel and the Arab countries of Egypt, Syria, and Jordan occurs, ending with Israel's victory

OCTOBER 2, 1967
Thurgood Marshall becomes the first Black Supreme Court Justice

APRIL 4, 1968
Martin Luther King Jr. is assassinated in Memphis, Tennessee

DECEMBER 3, 1967
Dr. Christiaan Barnard and his team perform the first human heart transplant in Cape Town, South Africa

JANUARY 20, 1969
Richard Nixon becomes the 37th president of the U.S.

NOVEMBER 10, 1969
The children's show *Sesame Street* premieres on PBS

MARCH 16, 1968
U.S. troops enter the Vietnamese village of My Lai and commit war crimes against civilians in what becomes known as the My Lai massacre

OCTOBER 16, 1968
Gold medalist Tommie Smith and bronze medalist John Carlos give the Black Power salute during a medal ceremony at the Summer Olympics

JULY 20, 1969
Neil Armstrong and Edwin "Buzz" Aldrin walk on the Moon

GLOSSARY

assassinated—murdered in a sudden attack for political reasons

British Invasion—a cultural phenomenon in the mid-1960s when British rock music became popular in the U.S.

carnage—the excessive and savage killing of many people, especially in battle

charisma—a personal quality that makes someone appealing and influential

Cold War—a conflict between the U.S. and the Soviet Union in the second half of the 1900s that did not break out into fighting

colonial—related to the practice of extending and maintaining a nation's political and economic control over another people or area

command module—a detachable part of a spacecraft that provides living quarters, a control center, and communications equipment for the crew

communism—a social system in which property and goods are controlled by the government

counterculture—values and ways of life that differ from what society considers normal or typical

discrimination—the act of treating someone unfairly because of race, gender, age, or other differences

draft—a system for selecting individuals from a group without their consent for military service

entrenched—firmly established and difficult to change

genres—categories of a kind of art based on style, form, or content

icons—widely admired, influential persons or things that are considered symbols of something in a particular area

immunization—treatments to create immunity to diseases

integrated circuits—small, electronic chips that contain many interconnected parts; integrated circuits are typically made from a wafer of silicon.

LGBTQ+—a community of people who identify as something other than heterosexual or the gender they were assigned at birth; LGBTQ+ stands for Lesbian, Gay, Bisexual, Transgender, Queer and other identities.

lunar module—a spacecraft that carries astronauts from the command module to the surface of the Moon and back

nuclear war—a conflict with nuclear weapons; nuclear weapons are extremely powerful and can produce destruction quickly with long-lasting effects.

overhead projectors—pieces of equipment that use light and a mirror to project images on a transparency onto a wall or screen

persecution—cruel and unfair treatment, especially toward those who differ in religion, race, or beliefs

psychedelic—relating to the period of the mid- to late-1960s that is associated with the counterculture

racism—the belief that race is a fundamental part of human traits and that certain races are superior to others

sit-ins—non-violent protests where people occupy spaces to demand change

Soviet Union—short for the Union of Soviet Socialist Republics; the Soviet Union is a former country in Eastern Europe and western Asia made up of 15 republics or states that broke up in 1991.

turbulence—a state of disorder or unrest

WRITE ABOUT IT!

- Imagine you were the first person to step foot on the Moon. **What would you say?**

- Is there a form of activism from the 1960s that you strongly agree or disagree with? **What is it? Why?**

- Is there an event or technology from the 1960s that continues to affect life today? **Why?**

ALSO CHECK OUT

INDEX

The images in this book are reproduced through the courtesy of: Bill Waterson/ Alamy Stock Photo, front cover (Martin Luther King Jr.), p. 9 (assassinations); Nutkamol komolvanich, front cover (Super Moon); Smith Archive/ Alamy Stock Photo, front cover (Muhammad Ali); Everett Collection Historical/ Alamy Stock Photo, front cover (demonstrators), p. 8 (President Kennedy); PictureLux/ The Hollywood Archive/ Alamy Stock Photo, front cover (The Brady Bunch), p. 35 (The Flintstones); Uber Bilder/ Alamy Stock Photo, front cover (Marvel Comic); Vic Stein/ AP Newsroom, front cover (NFL); Allstar Picture Library Limited./ Alamy Stock Photo, pp. 3 (Sesame Street), 33 (Mary Poppins), 35 (Sesame Street); NASA/ Wikipedia, pp. 3 (Neil Armstrong), 13 (Neil Armstrong), 42 (February 1962); Bettmann/ Contributor/ Getty Images, pp. 3 (March on Washington), 19 (March on Washington), 10, 14 (cultural revolution), 17 (U.S. soldiers), 18, 19 (all), 23 (warning on cigarette packages), 34 (debate), 39 (Sandy Koufax, Vince Lombardi), 40 (U.S.), 43 (February 1964), 44 (January 1969); Michael Ochs Archives/ Stringer/ Getty Images, pp. 3 (Bob Dylan), 37 (Bob Dylan); Wirestock | Dreamstime.com, p. 4 (station wagon); Archive Photos/ Stringer/ Getty Images, p. 4 (Ed Sullivan); Everett Collection Inc/ Alamy Stock Photo, p. 4 (fans); Mirrorpix/ Contributor/ Getty Images, pp. 5, 15 (Berlin Wall); SP–design, p. 6; Winai Tepsuttinun, p. 7 (gas); Artiom Photo, p. 7 (milk); Photo Builder, p. 7 (newspaper); phive2015, p. 7 (bread); AlenKadr, p. 7 (Coke); MPI/ Stringer/ Getty Images, p. 8 (Cuban Missile Crisis); New York Daily News Archive/ Contributor/ Getty Images, p. 8 (Stonewall Uprising); S.Sgt. Albert R. Simpson/ Wikipedia, p. 9 (Vietnam War); Ted Streshinsky Photographic Archive/ Contributor/ Getty Images, p. 9 (Summer of Love); Paul Conklin/ Contributor/ Getty Images, p. 11 (Peace Corps); Photo 12/ Contributor/ Getty Images, pp. 11 (Johnson), 23 (Dr. Sabin); PhotoQuest/ Contributor/ Getty Images, p. 11 (Black voters); Print Collector/ Contributor/ Getty Images, p. 12; wertinio, p. 13 (flag); tim page/ Contributor/ Getty Images, p. 14 (Palestinians); Historical/ Contributor/ Getty Images, p. 14 (Outer Space Treaty); Sovfoto/ Contributor/ Getty Images, p. 15 (Mao Zedong); Leif Skoogfors/ Contributor/ Getty Images, p. 16; FPG/ Staff/ Getty Images, p. 17 (girl with sign); -/ Contributor/ Getty Images, pp. 17 (North Vietnam), 43 (June 1963); Pictures from History/ Contributor/ Getty Images, p. 17 (spraying chemicals); Apic/ Contributor/ Getty Images, p. 20; Joerg Boethling/ Alamy Stock Photo, p. 21; Daily Herald Archive/ Contributor/ Getty Images, p. 22 (The Pill); Mondadori Portfolio/ Contributor/ Getty Images, p. 22 (Dr. Christiaan Barnard); Popperfoto/ Contributor/ Getty Images, pp. 23 (Washkansky), 26, 27 (The Beatles); KATERYNA KON/ SCIENCE PHOTO LIBRARY/ Getty Images, p. 23 (measles virus); Pictorial Press Ltd/ Alamy Stock Photo, pp. 24 (McDonald's), 44 (1965); North Carolina Central University/ Contributor/ Getty Images, p. 24 (overhead projector); Allan Cash Picture Library/ Alamy Stock Photo, p. 24 (women graduating college); Anthony Barboza/ Contributor/ Getty Images, p. 27 (Afro); Universal History Archive/ Contributor/ Getty Images, p. 27 (Jacqueline Kennedy); Monitor Picture Library/ Contributor/ Getty Images, p. 27 (Jimi Hendrix); Drew Gardner/ Alamy Stock Photo, p. 28 (Etch A Sketch); Chris Willson/ Alamy Stock Photo, pp. 28 (G.I. Joe), 29 (Easy-Bake Oven, Hot Wheels); Chris McNair/ Contributor/ Getty Images, p. 29 (Chatty Cathy); The Protected Art Archive/ Alamy Stock Photo, p. 30; Full dust jacket/ Wikipedia, p. 31 (Charlie and the Chocolate Factory); Ngaiman Dowe, p. 31 (Marvel Comics); Shawshots/ Alamy Stock Photo, p. 32 (musicals); Photo 12/ Alamy Stock Photo, p. 32 (2001: A Space Odyssey); Sueddeutsche Zeitung Photo/ Alamy Stock Photo, p. 33 (James Bond Franchise); Allstar Picture Library Ltd/ Alamy Stock Photo, p. 33 (One Hundred and One Dalmatians); Silver Screen Collection/ Contributor/ Getty Images, pp. 34 (The Andy Griffith Show), 43 (August 1962); Sunset Boulevard/ Contributor/ Getty Images, p. 35 (Star Trek); Howard Arnold Collection/ Contributor/ Getty Images, p. 36; ullstein bild Dtl./ Contributor/ Getty Images, p. 37 (The Beatles); Charlie Gillett Collection/ Contributor/ Getty Images, p. 37 (The Supremes); Archive PL/ Alamy Stock Photo, p. 38; Focus On Sport/ Contributor/ Getty Images, p. 39 (Muhammad Ali); Jerry Cooke/ Contributor/ Getty Images, p. 40 (Mexico); David Lees/ Contributor/ Getty Images, p. 40 (Italy); Robert Riger/ Contributor/ Getty Images, p. 40 (France); Rolls Press/ Popperfoto/ Contributor/ Getty Images, p. 40 (Austria); Keystone-France/ Contributor/ Getty Images, pp. 40 (Japan), 41 (judo); Ed Lacey/ Popperfoto/ Contributor/ Getty Images, p. 41 (Rod Laver); PA Images/ Contributor/ Getty Images, p. 41 (Francis Chichester); Glasshouse Images/ Alamy Stock Photo, p. 42 (September 1962); Janvier, p. 44 (April 1966); Michael Ochs Archives/ Handout/ Getty Images, p. 44 (July 1969); Album/ Alamy Stock Photo, p. 44 (November 1969).